My Favorite Machine
AMBULANCES

Victoria Marcos

xist Publishing

Published in the United States by Xist Publishing
www.xistpublishing.com
PO Box 61593 Irvine, CA 92602

© 2019 Text by Victoria Marcos
All images licensed from Fotolia & Adobe Stock
All rights reserved
No portion of this book may be reproduced without
express permission of the publisher

First Edition
Hardcover ISBN:978-1-5324-1240-0
Paperback ISBN: 978-1-5324-1237-0
eISBN: 978-1-5324-1237-0

Table of Contents

Let's Learn about Ambulances 4
What does an Ambulance do? 8
Do You Remember 12

How does an Ambulance work? 15
Do You Remember 20

Types of Ambulances 24
Do You Remember 30

Your Favorite Thing 33
Glossary 34
Answers 35

My favorite machines are ambulances.

Would you like to learn about them?

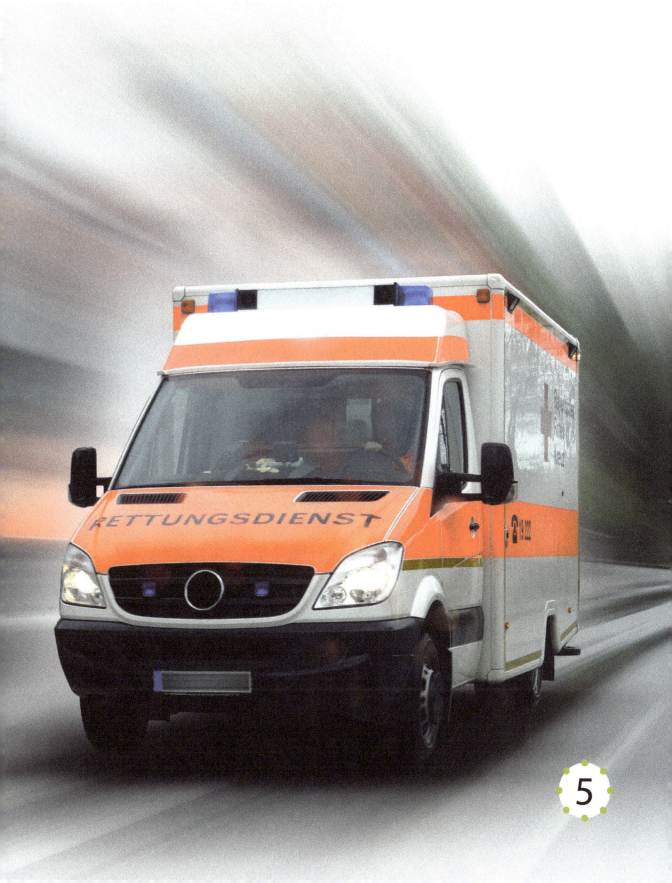

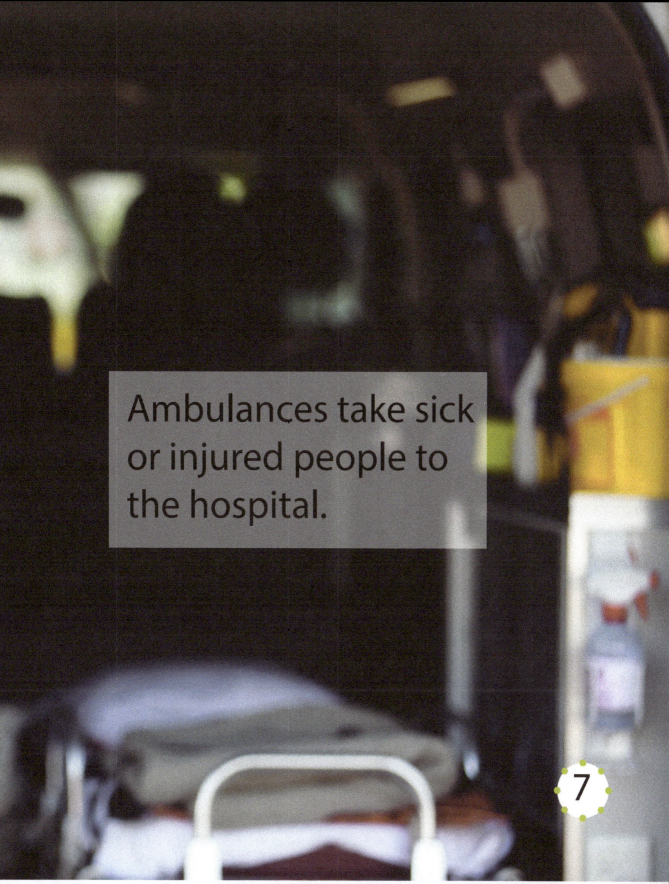

Ambulances take sick or injured people to the hospital.

One paramedic drives while the other helps the patient until they reach the hospital.

Ambulances have equipment and medicines that paramedics use to treat the patient.

Do You Remember?

What is an ambulance used for?

Check and see if you're right at the end of this book!

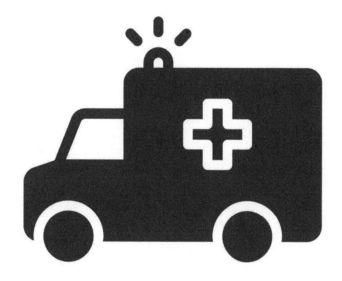

Ambulances use loud sirens, so drivers know to get out of their way.

They also use flashing lights to warn other drivers.

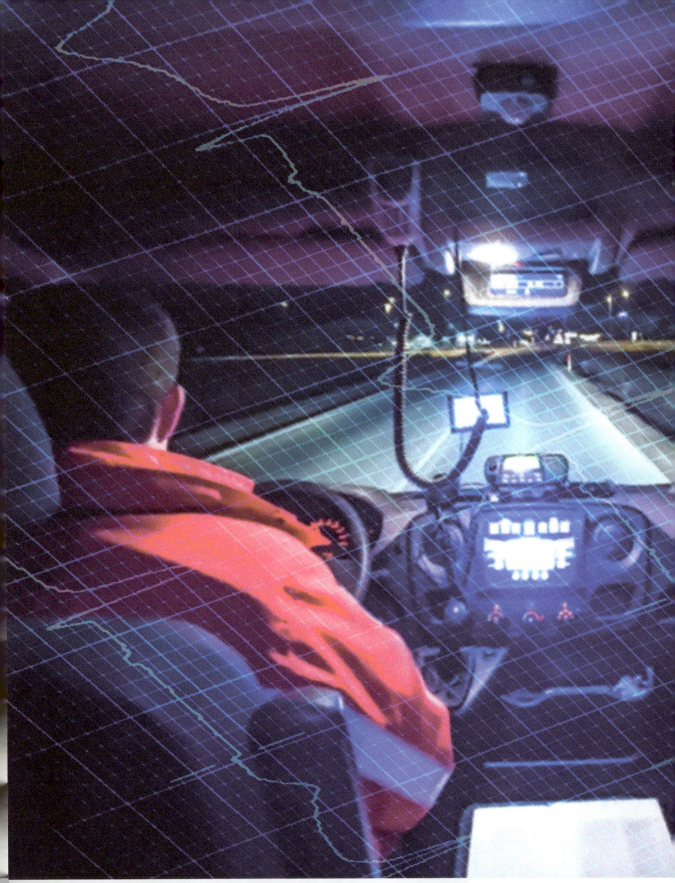

Ambulances have two-way radios that paramedics use to communicate with the hospital.

Do You Remember?

What do ambulances use to warn drivers?

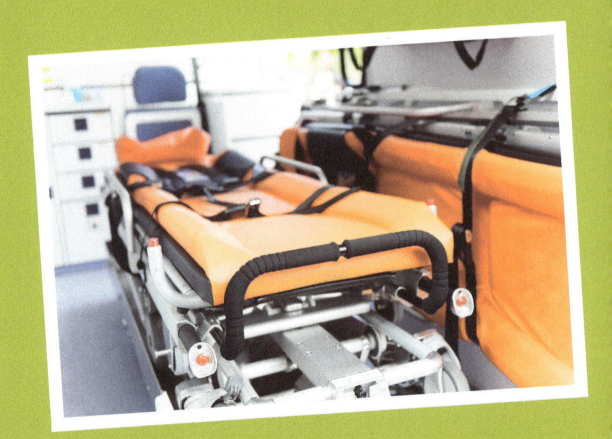

Check and see if you're right at the end of this book!

Paramedics use a gurney to take the patient in and out of the ambulance.

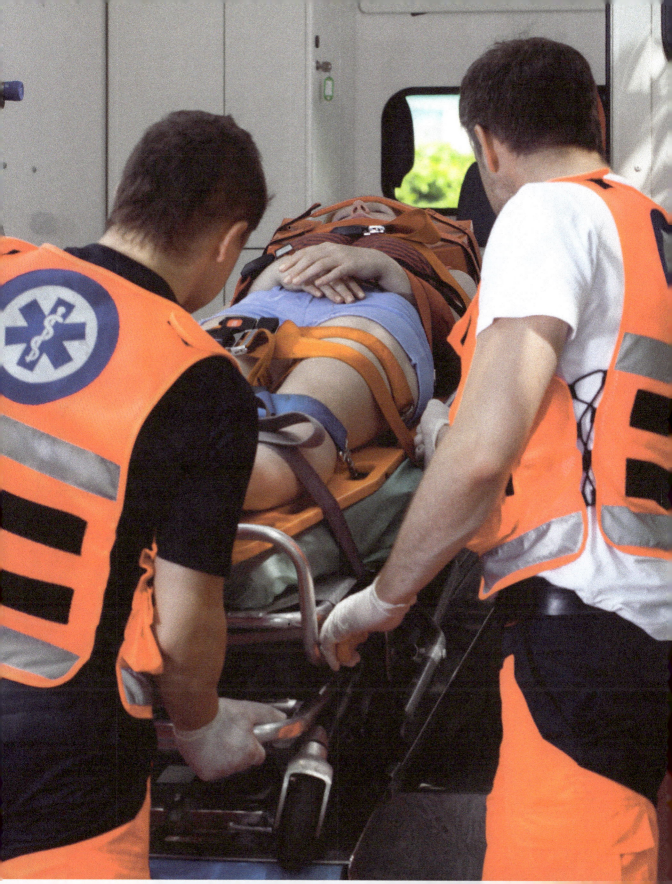

Ambulances can be trucks, SUVs, boats, helicopters, or other vehicles.

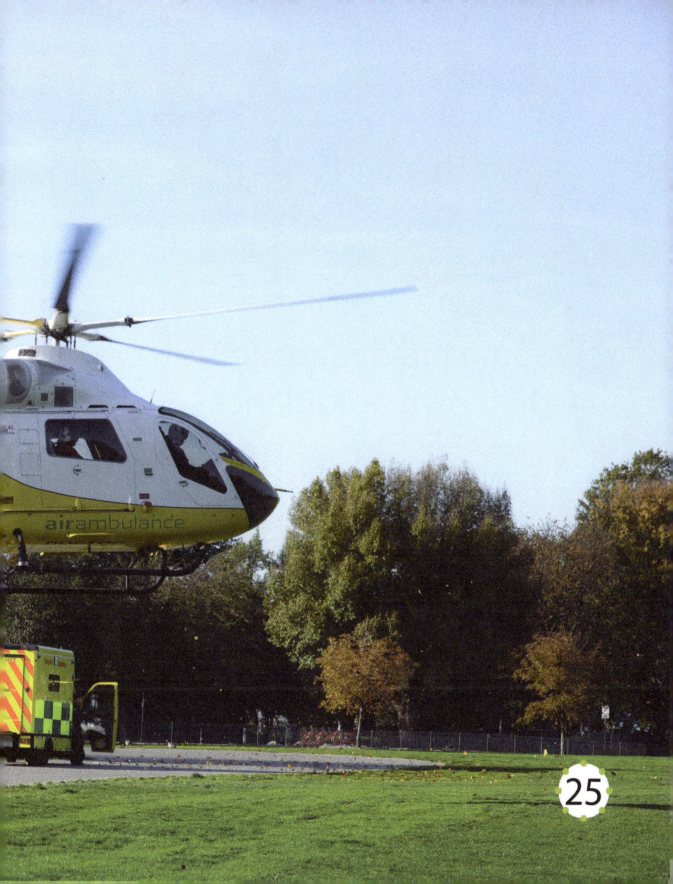

Some fire departments have their own ambulances.

Most ambulances are emergency ambulances.

Do You Remember?

What is the most common type of ambulance?

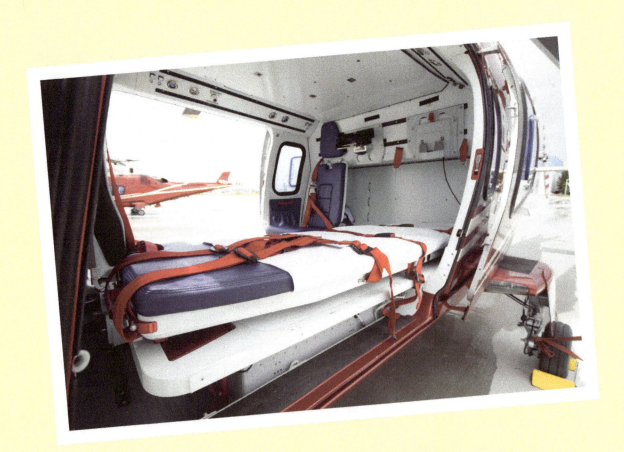

30

Check and see if you're right at the end of this book!

What is your favorite thing about ambulances?

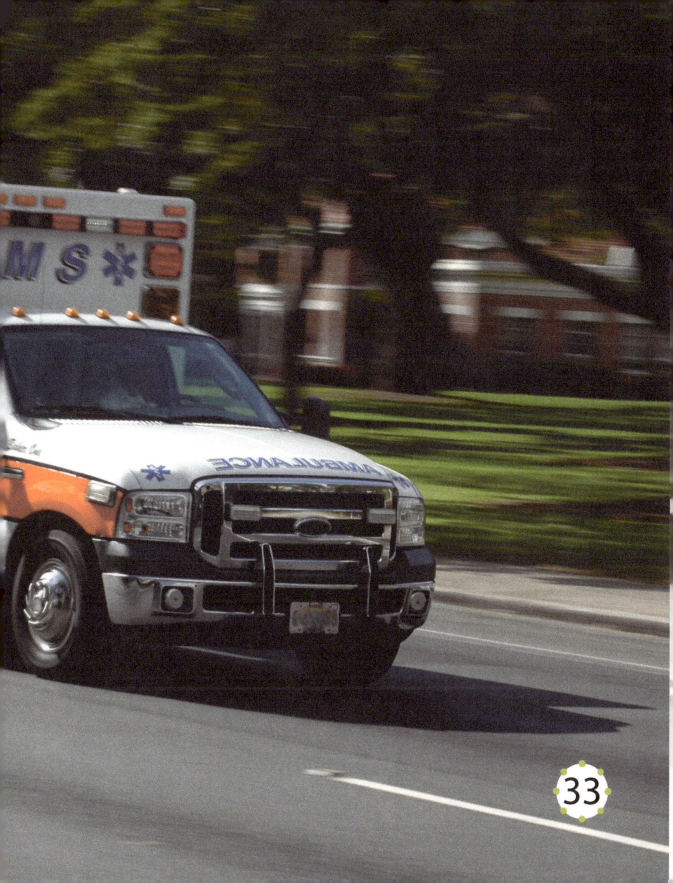

Glossary

Injured: Hurt

Paramedic: A person that gives emergency medical care to patients before they are taken to the hospital

Equipment: Tools that are used for a specific purpose

Gurney: A bed with wheels used to transport patients

Two-way radio: A radio that two people can use to talk to each other

Did You Remember?

Answers:
Question #1:
To take sick and injured people to the hospital.
Question #2:
Sirens and flashing lights.
Question #3:
An emergency ambulance.

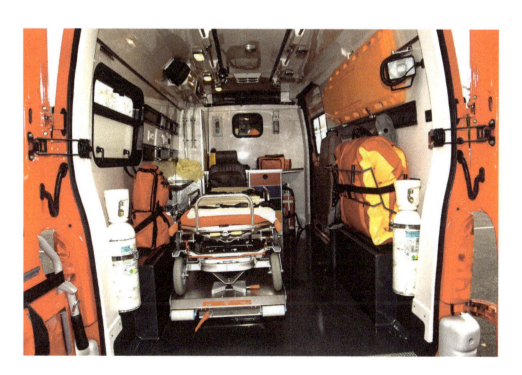

CPSIA information can be obtained
at www.ICGtesting.com
Printed in the USA
LVHW071551150420
653471LV00001B/48